HUMANPOWER

ROGER YEPSEN

HUMANPOWER

Cars, Planes, and Boats with Muscles for Motors

Macmillan Publishing Company   New York

Maxwell Macmillan Canada   Toronto

Maxwell Macmillan International
New York   Oxford   Singapore   Sydney

Illustrations on pages 10, 12, 14, and 15 reprinted with
permission from *Bicycles and Tricycles* by Archibald Sharp,
copyright 1977 by MIT Press. Illustration on page 11 reprinted
with permission from *Bicycle Science* by Frank Rowland Whitt
and David Gordon, copyright 1980 by MIT Press. Illustrations
on pages 25 and 26 reprinted with permission from *The History
of Man-Powered Flight* by D. A. Reay.

Macmillan Publishing Company is part of the
Maxwell Communication Group of Companies.
Macmillan Publishing Company
866 Third Avenue, New York, NY 10022
Maxwell Macmillan Canada, Inc.
1200 Eglinton Avenue East, Suite 200
Don Mills, Ontario M3C 3N1
First edition
Printed in the United States of America

10   9   8   7   6   5   4   3   2   1
The text of this book is set in 13 point ITC Garamond Light.
Book design by Constance Ftera

Library of Congress Cataloging-in-Publication Data
Yepsen, Roger B.
Humanpower : cars, planes, and boats with muscles for
motors / by Roger Yepsen.—1st ed.
p.   cm.
Includes bibliographical references and index.
Summary: Describes and provides the history for a variety
of vehicles that run on human muscle power.
ISBN 0-02-793615-5
1. Human powered vehicles—Juvenile literature.
[1. Human powered vehicles.]   I. Title.
TL147.Y44 1992   629.04′6—dc20   91-17575

This book is for my youngest pedaler,
Rhodes

Contents

1. The Exciting (and Sometimes Silly) History of Humanpowered Travel

Humanpowered vehicles are nothing new. It seems that people have *always* been trying to go faster with their own muscle power.

Kiddy Cars for Grown-Ups

The first humanpowered vehicles on land didn't travel much faster than you can walk. One of them was a carriage used by people lucky enough to have a servant who would operate the foot pedals.

And then in 1817, a German inventor named Karl von Drais found a way to go faster. He discovered that if you go fast enough

On Karl von Drais's running machine, a rider could average up to 10 miles per hour.

on a two-wheeler, you can take your feet off the ground *without tipping over*.

That doesn't sound like much of a brainstorm, does it? But many great discoveries are really very simple. Von Drais entered races against runners and even horse-drawn mail carriages, and he won. Although he could only creep up hills, he lifted his feet and zoomed down the other side. Von Drais may have been the world's fastest human during the early 1800s. Before long many people were trying his daring method of coasting down-hill. Driver-education schools were opened to teach them how.

Still, von Drais's running machine wasn't a very practical way of getting around. It was great fun racing downhill, but a chore creeping back up. People needed a better way to use their power than pushing with their feet. Running machines didn't make good use of the rider's muscles.

A Scottish blacksmith named Kirkpatrick Macmillan came up with a vehicle that did. In 1839 he tried attaching a pair of cranks to the rear wheel of his running machine. The result was the world's first true bicycle. Crowds turned out to watch Macmillan speed past. He soon made history again—by accidentally knocking down a spectator and receiving the world's first traffic ticket!

And then the world forgot about Macmillan and his amazing

Kirkpatrick Macmillan's pedal-powered running machine was the world's first bicycle.

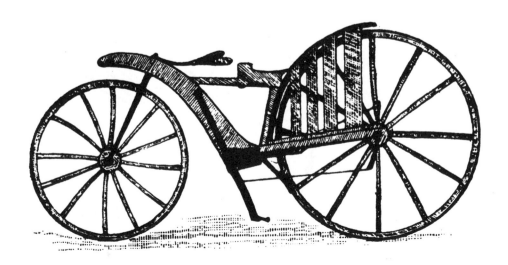

machine. It took another invention to turn bicycling into a craze. Again, the idea was simple: to stick pedals on the front wheel, just like today's tricycles.

You know the problem with that idea if you remember how fast you have to spin the pedals on a tricycle. But bike builders found a way around this. They made the front wheel bigger. And bigger and bigger. The larger the wheel, the farther a bike would go with each turn of the pedals.

The Hair-Raising Highwheeler

Front wheels continued to grow as bike riders became hungry for more speed. The fastest bikes looked ridiculous, with wheels over five feet high. These extremely tippy bikes were called highwheelers, a name they deserved.

Only very rugged people enjoyed riding highwheelers. A

It took a brave rider to risk sitting way up on the seat of a highwheeler.

12

fall from that height could break an arm or crack a skull. A rider also had to be *tall* (to reach the pedals on that huge wheel) and *male* (a highwheeler couldn't be ridden in a skirt, and women of that time were rarely seen in pants). It's not surprising that many people gave up on bicycles. They turned to another way of traveling fast, one that allowed them to stay a lot closer to the ground—roller-skating. It became a national fad in the United States in the 1870s.

Meanwhile, inventors kept on tinkering with the bicycle. By the 1880s they had come up with a new way of making a bike go fast. It's a method used on your own bicycle today—running a chain between the pedals and one of the wheels.

Have you noticed that the chain goes around a big sprocket at the pedal end and around a smaller sprocket at the wheel end? This allows the pedals to turn more slowly than the back wheel.

Bikes with chains didn't need that huge front wheel. The rider could stay closer to the ground. That, of course, was a good place to be in an accident, and the new machines were called "safety bicycles." Safety may be smart, but some people pretend they don't care about it. The tough highwheeler cyclists made fun of these low, easy-to-ride bikes, calling them dwarfs.

The Modern Bicycle

The safety bicycles were fast. For the energy it took to walk just 4 miles per hour, a bike rider could pedal 16. But the new bikes were as bumpy as the old highwheelers, until another invention came along—the air-filled tire. Here was another good idea that sounded simple. Black, air-filled rubber dough-

*A safety bicycle, 1890. The bike has changed little
in more than a hundred years.*

nuts were attached to the wheels in order to soak up shocks
before they reached the rider.

The highwheeler riders said the new tires were wimpy, of
course, and insisted on calling them sausages. But in races, the
"dwarf" bikes on their "sausages" managed to zip right past the
tall, dangerous bikes. Before long, highwheelers disappeared
from the road. The safety bicycle became the most popular
vehicle in the world.

The 1890s were the golden age of the bicycle. People used
them to get to work, to carry freight, to deliver mail, and to go
into battle, as well as to just ride for fun. Inventors turned out
strange and wonderful machines: ten-person cycles, dog-pow-
ered cycles, humanpowered plows for farmers, and one-
wheeled cycles with the rider seated *inside* the wheel. Thousands of people even glided over railroad tracks with specially

equipped machines. A bicycle railroad was built between two towns in New Jersey. Bikes ran on a single rail like little train cars.

In the United States, bicycle racing had as many fans as baseball. Racetracks for bikes, called velodromes, were built in towns all over the country. The best-known American racer was a black man named Major Taylor. He was one of the first superstars of any sport. Taylor not only won many championships but also cycled twice around the world.

In the 1800s, people rode monocycles (with one wheel) and quadricycles (with four), as well as bikes and trikes. Left: This monocycle had two riders. Right: This quadricycle could accommodate a passenger in back.

Above: A group rides into the countryside on rail bikes.
Below: A fire warden patrols on his rail vehicle.

The golden age of the bicycle didn't last long. People fell in love with faster ways of getting around—the automobile, and then the airplane. By 1910 the bicycle was no longer an important way to travel in the United States. Adults came to think of it as a child's toy, like a sled or a scooter. Most velodromes were torn down. Major Taylor became the forgotten star of a forgotten sport. He died a poor man and was buried in an unmarked grave. It would be many years before bicycles again caused much excitement in the United States.

Paddle Power

Boats were the very first humanpowered vehicles. Back when the world had no smooth roads or sidewalks, rivers and seas were the fastest way of getting around. The most powerful

This bicycle railroad looks like a great idea.
But it was abandoned in 1898, after only six years.

humanpowered vehicle of all time was the trireme, an ancient Mediterranean warship propelled by as many as *one thousand* rowers!

Early boats were used for the serious business of travel, fighting, and exploring. But by the 1800s, many people had discovered that boats could be fun, too. Builders began making fast, lightweight canoes and rowboats.

One canoeist became famous for paddling hundreds of miles in the lightest canoes of all. He called himself Nesmuk, but he was actually a shoemaker named George Washington Sears—an awfully long name for a tiny and often sickly man. Nesmuk's boats measured about ten feet long and weighed as little as ten pounds. With their delicate, fingerlike ribs, they looked like a cross between a bat wing and a pea pod.

A museum director has no trouble lifting one of Nesmuk's featherweight boats, the Wee Lassie.

This European watercycle of the 1860s
was built for comfort, not for speed.

Inspired by Nesmuk, builders made lighter, sleeker canoes
and rowboats that broke many speed records. They tried putting
pedals on boats, too. Pedal-powered boats were known as watercycles. They were odd-looking things, but they quickly won
a lot of fans.

The paddle and the oar are simple devices to push water
backward and a boat forward; they've done a good job for thousands of years. But a watercycle uses a propeller to get more
speed from the same amount of work. It can be driven by the
powerful muscles of the legs, too, leaving your hands free to
steer. And unlike in a rower, you pedal facing forward, so that
you can see where you're going!

Watercycles broke all sorts of speed records set by canoes
and rowboats. With several pedalers on board, they could travel
an amazing 15 miles per hour. But the motorboat made the

watercycle look like it was standing still. Pedal-powered boats disappeared. Watercycles would again break world humanpowered speed records, but not until well into the next century. People continued to row and paddle in boats that remained almost the same, year after year.

Attack of the Killer Turtle

One of the most interesting propeller-driven boats traveled where no boat had gone before—under the water. The *Turtle* was the world's very first submarine. It wasn't much more than a wooden keg with propellers sticking out of it. But the *Turtle* had been built by David Bushnell for a big job: to attack the British warships that had taken control of New York Harbor during the Revolutionary War.

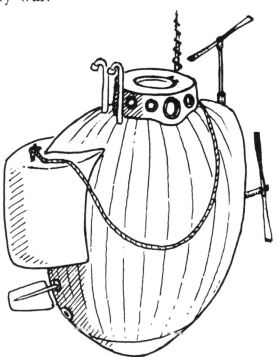

The humanpowered Turtle *was the first submarine in the world. It probably was the cutest, too.*

20

One evening a colonial soldier named Ezra Lee climbed into the tiny keg and pulled the lid shut. He spun a hand crank attached to a propeller and slowly crossed the harbor. His target was the *Eagle*, a 64-gun British warship that was keeping American ships out of New York.

As Lee approached the ship, he opened a valve that let seawater into the submarine. The *Turtle* sank out of sight. Lee edged closer until he felt a bump. He jabbed a large screw into the *Eagle* and turned a crank that would attach the bomb that the *Turtle* carried. But the screw didn't take hold. And the bomb was ticking. Soon it would explode. Just as bad, Lee had used up nearly all the air in his cramped cabin.

He spun the propeller to get away from the ship, pumped out enough water to bob to the surface, and spun his ventilator fan to bring in fresh air.

As Ezra Lee raced to shore, he released the bomb to make better speed. An enemy ship spotted the bomb and came closer to look—just as it blew up. The ship wasn't damaged, but the British were so amazed that they gave up chasing American ships from the harbor. Without hurting a single person, the *Turtle* had won its battle.

Humans with Wings

When you were younger, you probably ran around flapping your arms and pretending you could fly. Many adults have dreamed of being free from Earth's gravity, too. They've been building machines designed to fly by humanpower for centuries. They've also been *crashing* for centuries.

The best-known crash of all was supposed to have hap-

This picture of a winged flyer is based on an invention patented in 1889. These stubby wings couldn't really have lifted a person above the ground. Humanpowered flight remained a dream until the 1970s.

pened around 3500 B.C. in the Mediterranean Sea. An inventor, Daedalus, and his son, Icarus, escaped from an island prison on wings that Daedalus had made of feathers and wax. But young Icarus flew higher and higher, in spite of his father's warnings that the sun's heat would melt the wax and loosen the feathers. Icarus fell into the sea and drowned.

That story is just a fable. But throughout history, people have built contraptions made of feathers, silk, and wood in attempts to fly with their own power. Unlike Icarus, they didn't get very far from the ground. Even Leonardo da Vinci, the brilliant Italian artist and inventor, could do no better. Five hundred years ago, he sketched designs for humanpowered planes and a helicopter. But it seems that they never got off the drawing board.

Countless others have tried and failed. Some broke bones, and some lost their lives. Several years before Columbus set off for America, another bold Italian, John Baptist Danti, climbed a tower and set off through the air with winged oars. He crashed on a church roof and was seriously injured.

In the 1500s, John Damian attempted to race a sailing ship from Scotland to France. Needless to say, he lost. Flapping a pair of wings made from chicken feathers, he leaped from a castle wall and went straight down, breaking his thigh bone.

In Germany in the 1600s, a cautious man named Bernier tested his flying machine by jumping first from a stool, then a table, a first-floor window, and a second-floor window. He should have stopped there. His last leap, from a third-floor window, resulted in several broken bones.

In the 1800s, Belgian shoemaker Vincent de Groof used his skills to make an *ornithopter*—an airplane that flies like a bird. The wings were operated by his arms, while his legs flapped a tail. He launched himself from a balloon and fell to his death.

Were these people foolish to try such stunts? Or would you call them brave pioneers? Today, when men and women are killed in attempts to explore space, we consider them heroes, not fools.

Pedaling Pilots

Experts looked at this dismal record and declared that humans would never share the skies with birds and bats. But the experts were wrong.

Plane designers were getting closer. In the 1800s they began to realize they would have to pay closer attention to animals that *can* fly. But it's difficult to get close enough to birds to study them. Russian researchers found a clever solution to that problem. They froze dead birds until stiff, then dropped them from kites to watch how they glided back to earth.

Designers also began making experiments with models, rather than risking their lives in full-sized planes. Then when it came time to test real planes, they used weighted dummies instead of living pilots.

One of the most serious designers of the 1800s was Otto Lilienthal, a German who built an ornithopter while still a student. He practiced wing-flapping exercises—at night, to avoid being laughed at by his school friends. When it came time to test his flying machine, Lilienthal didn't take unnecessary chances. He hung the contraption from the beams of a roof.

But Lilienthal wasn't able to fly. Neither could any other

Above: Humanpowered planes competed for a French prize in 1912. This contestant gets a little help from a ramp. Below: To win the prize, a plane had to fly over wires strung across the track. This pilot rolled right over them.

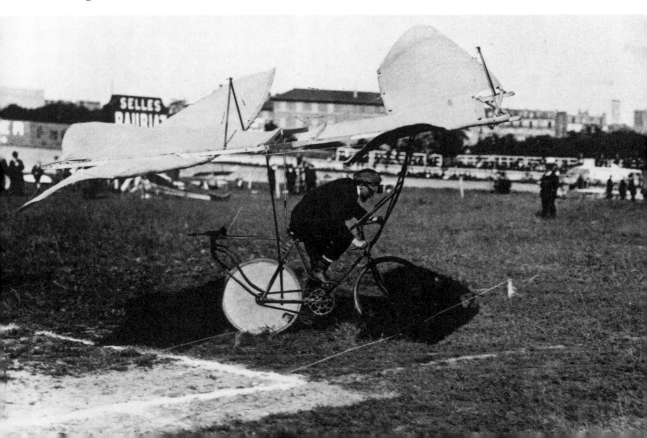

*The well-dressed pilot of this ornithopter failed
to flap his way to the 1912 prize.*

experimenters. The Wright brothers' motor-powered plane took
off in 1903, yet humanpowered pilots continued to fly about as
well as penguins.

Still, many of them kept on flapping and pedaling. They
got some encouragement in 1912, when a French car manufac-
turer offered a large prize for the first humanpowered flight.

Ninety planes tried to win the prize. Not a single one managed to fly.

Some of these planes weren't much more than bicycles with wings strapped on. Other pilots tried the old-fashioned method of flapping their way to the prize in ornithopters.

The best of the designs used a propeller to push the plane after it left the ground. It was one of these machines that finally captured the prize, nine years later. The winner, a Frenchman named Gabriel Poulain, called his machine an aerocycle. Even though his "flight" was only a hop of forty feet, Poulain boldly claimed that someday all of us would have our own aerocycles.

These planes were clumsy because they didn't give their hard-working pilots enough help in beating the forces that held them to the ground—gravity and friction against the air. Human flight would have to wait until designers could come up with streamlined planes made of light, strong, space-age materials.

Muscles and Motors

So you can see that humanpowered bikes, boats, and planes ran into a big wall. Not a real wall, but something that slowed them down just about as well—the gasoline engine. That hot, noisy little box could take a sip of fuel and turn it into a horse barn full of power. Suddenly the human body seemed almost helplessly weak. Why bother with pedals and paddles and oars—and sweat—when an engine could do the job ten or a hundred times better?

2. *Humanpowered Cars*

The bicycle has been frozen in time. Your own bike doesn't look much different than the hundred-year-old safety bike shown in Chapter 1. And yet we can barely recognize many other machines from those horse-and-buggy days.

There are two reasons the bike hasn't changed much in a century. One, as we've already seen, was the automobile. As soon as this loud, fast, and shiny machine came along, most adults left their bicycles in the garage. Inventors chose to work with cars, and later with airplanes, rather than with the handful of parts that make up a bicycle.

And the second reason? The story behind that one begins on a bicycle racetrack in France more than fifty years ago.

Francois Faure's Illegal Bicycle

In the 1930s, a French cyclist named Francois Faure showed up for a race on a contraption called a Velocar. It was long and low. Faure rode it in what is known as a recumbent position—

leaning way back, with his feet out in front and his head over the rear wheel. The idea was to slip through the air more easily than riders sitting up on regular racing bikes. The bike looked odd. But Francois Faure broke nearly every record in the books.

Other bicycle racers weren't happy. The International Cycling Union, which ran bicycle races around the world, made a rule that bikes be at least a certain height. The Union also

Francois Faure, shown at the right on his Velocar, prepares for a race. The Velocar was so fast that it was soon banned from official races.

The Vector is a streamlined tricycle that goes fast enough to keep up with highway traffic. Photo © 1981 by Randa Bishop.

banned streamlining. These two rules helped to kill any enthusiasm inventors had for turning the bicycle into a new and faster machine. Speed records remained unchanged for many years.

But now the bicycle is evolving again. As gasoline gets more expensive and pollution becomes a greater threat, inventors are once more trying to make fast, practical, humanpowered vehicles. International rules still ban low, streamlined bikes from official races. So in many countries streamlined riders have set up their own races and record books. The vehicles don't all look the same, as they do in a regular bicycle race. There are silvery cigars, tall fins, and soft cocoons. But all have one thing in common—they go very fast, fast enough to break highway speed limits.

Pedaling Past the Speed Limit

A tiny yellow car pulls onto a busy California interstate highway. Its two passengers look out through a bubblelike window.

The car accelerates to better than 50 miles per hour, making barely a sound. People in other vehicles stare, and not only because the little car is less than a yard high and rides on just three wheels.

The oddest thing about this car is that the passengers are *pedaling*. At 50 miles per hour, they are just cruising comfortably. In a sprint, they can do close to 70!

A one-person vehicle, the *Gold Rush*, has gone over 65 miles per hour. That's faster than a single human has ever traveled under his or her own power. And no one expects the record to stay at 65 for long.

The record-breaking Gold Rush *is in the collection of the National Museum of American History in Washington, D.C.*

Humanpowered cars are not only fast but quiet and energy efficient. They run on pennies worth of food and water—the passengers' fuel, in other words. This is the kind of fuel that empties refrigerators, not the world's oil supplies. And humanpowered cars don't pollute the environment with smoke and noise.

What does it feel like to pedal a low, streamlined humanpowered vehicle (or HPV)? Imagine hopping into one for a ride around the neighborhood. You'd stay dry in the rain and warm in the winter. Angry dogs couldn't snap at your sneakers. There would be storage space for your things. Even if you weren't in the greatest shape, you could pedal close to 40 miles per hour for a block or two. That's fast enough to get you a speeding ticket in some parts of town. You wouldn't even need to be old enough for a driver's license—just big enough to reach the pedals!

So why isn't every kid on the block riding an HPV? What's keeping *you* from going right out and buying one at the local cycle shop?

First of all, you probably won't find one there. The big bike companies still make only ordinary bicycles. Second, HPVs cost a lot of money. The fastest ones may be as expensive as cars. And price isn't the only thing that keeps them off the road.

The streamlined shell can cause a number of difficulties. It's tricky just to climb inside. The shell tends to be stuffy, too, so that hard-working riders may feel like they are being steamed alive. Strong winds are another danger—they can turn the body of a streamlined HPV into a sail, blowing it out of control or even lifting it right off the ground.

Hills can be more work for a recumbent rider, lying back in an HPV. When you come to a hill on your bike, what do you do? Stand on the pedals in order to use the muscles of your arms and back. But you can't very well do that if you're lying down, and this keeps the recumbent rider from generating the power needed to climb hills at top speed.

So, for now, most of us will continue to choose the family car or a bicycle for trips to school and the market. But designers and inventors are working hard to make HPVs that we can use for everyday driving.

Air Is a Drag!

These designers and inventors are battling with something they can't even see—air. Air is the big enemy of a cyclist trying to go like the wind. It doesn't *seem* like much of a barrier. After all, it's invisible. But air is a "drag," technically speaking. Drag is another term for wind resistance.

At very slow speeds, a low and streamlined design doesn't help you much. But the faster you ride a bike, the harder it is to push through Earth's atmosphere. At 10 miles per hour, more than half of your muscle power is used to fight air resistance; at 20, three-quarters goes to pushing through the air; and around 30, which is top speed for most of us on a regular bike, the figure reaches 90 percent. If you could ride your bike on the moon, without all of that air to slow you down, you'd probably have no trouble pedaling at 200 miles per hour.

Cyclists do all sorts of things to escape drag. They try for new speed records on mile-high tracks, where thin air allows them to go up to 5 percent faster than at sea level. Stranger still, they also pedal behind speeding trains and cars that break the wind for them. In 1899 Charles "Mile-a-Minute" Murphy pedaled fast enough to justify his nickname—63 miles per hour—behind a speeding railroad train. Recently Allan Abbott, a California doctor whose hobby is racing HPVs on land and sea, rode a bike a record 138 miles per hour behind a car equipped to protect him from the wind.

This method, known as drafting, works for cyclists in races, too. You may have noticed that they gather in tight packs behind the leader, who helps to part the air for the rest. Drafting another cyclist can cut air resistance by half, but it is dangerous and you shouldn't try it. Riding behind a train isn't very practical either, of course. There are easier methods of cheating the wind.

Laid-back Bikers

The simplest way of reducing drag is to duck. If there are drop handlebars on your bike—the bent ones that look like a ram's horns—they'll allow you to ride in a lower position and cut down your wind resistance by at least 12 percent.

In the past few years, many bicyclists have switched to aero handlebars, which stick out in front of the bars the bike came with. Aero bars allow you to ride with your body low and your arms held as if you were about to make a clean dive into a pool. They can reduce your wind resistance another few percent.

A still better way to get out of the wind is to follow Francois Faure's example and lie down on a recumbent bike. This can chop wind resistance dramatically, by 20 percent and more. Of course, you need a special sort of bicycle to do that, and the bigger bike companies have yet to begin making them.

Recumbent bikes are ahead of their time, say the riders who like them. It seems that the world isn't always ready to grab new ideas. Remember, a hundred years ago, people made fun of the chain-drive safety bicycle, too.

Steering the Wind

Another way to slip through the wind more easily is to guide it right over you and your vehicle. This is known as streamlining.

The simplest place to start is your body. You can streamline

Above: This racer cuts air resistance on his recumbent bike. Photo © 1985 by Randa Bishop.   Below: You can also lessen wind drag by lying on your stomach. Photo © 1984 by Michael Chritton.

Two people can pedal faster than one. Photo © 1984 by Michael Chritton.

Here is a humanpower riddle: What has a big rear end and flies? A bicyclist wearing a tail cone. In the 1930s tests showed that a cone could increase a rider's top speed by 2 miles per hour.

your head end with the teardrop helmet worn by many racers. You can streamline your other end, too. In 1933 a Swiss bike builder named Oscar Egg invented a long cone that could be strapped to the rider's backside—if the rider didn't feel too foolish. Even though the cone really could make a cyclist go faster, Egg's idea never caught on.

Many bike riders dress in tight-fitting clothes. They not only look faster, but they waste less energy battling the wind than they would in baggy clothes.

Parts of the bike itself can be streamlined. Racers often use cone-shaped disks to cover the spokes, because spokes have been found to churn up the wind. Even the frame can be streamlined. You may have noticed bikes made of elliptical tubing: If you sawed through a pipe of the frame, you could see that it isn't round, but oval. This shape slips through the air more easily than the round tubing used on most bikes.

You can streamline the bike you have now by adding a curved plastic windshield, known as a fairing. It attaches to the handlebars, and it helps by directing the wind around your body. The larger the fairing, the more help it will be. The Zzipper fairing shown here should add roughly 1½ miles per hour to your top speed on level ground. (See chapter 5 for more information on streamlining a bike.)

This fairing not only protects you from the wind but also helps you cut through it.

Above: Streamlined HPVs slip through the wind better than ordinary bikes. Photo © 1984 by Michael Chritton. Below: In the 1930s, this streamlined Velocar became the first bicycle to travel 50 kilometers (about 31 miles) an hour.

Above: Pegasus, *a four-person tricycle, tears around a racetrack.*
Below: With its streamlined shell in place, Pegasus is even faster.

A racer is helped out of his vehicle after a crash. HPVs are built with speed in mind, not strength. Photo © 1984 by Michael Chritton.

One bike, the Lightning F-40, has a hard nose cone in front and a fairing of cloth that wraps right around the rider. Only the legs and head stick out. As wild as this cloth cocoon sounds, it's nothing new. A century ago, cyclists could buy a large cape with an inflatable rim that held the cloth in a streamlined shape.

The fastest HPVs are both recumbent *and* streamlined. They look like little rockets on wheels. The skins are smooth. The wheels can barely be seen. The result is a vehicle that slips through the air with as little wind resistance as the rear-view mirror of a tractor-trailer truck.

These machines are made as light as possible. Fractions of an ounce are shaved away by boring holes in some parts until they look like Swiss cheese. Another method is to use light-weight materials such as aluminum for the frames and fiberglass-and-foam sandwiches for the bodies. Some HPVs don't have frames at all. Instead, the wheels, controls, and other parts are bolted right to the body. The result is something like a clam, with the insides kept together by the shell.

Most HPVs are propelled with the legs, because these have the strongest muscles in the body. But others use the arms as well to add up to 20 percent more power. (See chapter 5 for information on handlebars that are rowed, something like the oars of a boat, to power the front wheel.) And one HPV, the Rowcycle, uses the arms only.

The Ellefson Rowcycle is rowed much like a boat; there are no pedals.

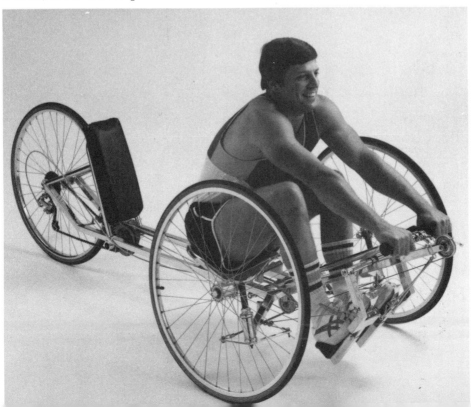

The Lightning F-40 *set a new record in the Race Across America.*

Getting Practical

Designers are now trying to make HPVs that not only go fast but are also safe and fun for everyday use around town. In fact, there are competitions that judge how well an HPV can carry bags of groceries or keep a rider dry in a rainstorm. And there are races to test how well an HPV can handle crowded highways and city streets, as well as racetracks safely lined with hay bales.

That's the idea behind the Race Across America. At 2,780 miles, this new bike race is the world's longest. A crew of four takes turns at the pedals, night and day. While one cyclist is riding, the others are traveling in a van, sleeping or eating in preparation for their turns.

In the first Race Across America, the leader for most of the trip was *Gold Rush America*. But the crew got lost near the end—their directions were sixty-four pages long—and they gave up. The winner was a Lightning F-40, which made the trip in only five days, one hour, and eight minutes. The F-40 isn't just fast; this HPV is practical enough that it is produced for sale—to anyone with $3,500 to spend on a bike, that is.

Humanpowered Trucks

In many parts of the world, humanpower is used to carry not only humans but cargo, too. The simplest vehicles are pulled and pushed by people on foot.

The Long Jan work bike is like a tiny pickup truck. It can carry 180 pounds of cargo.

All sorts of things can be carried in the bin of this recumbent German work bike.

Several companies make bicycles and tricycles that can carry up to 200 pounds of such cargo as groceries, pizzas, and packages. The Worksman Company sells its sturdy truck trike to restaurants that deliver food and to factories that need a cheap, quiet way to move things about. Hundreds of them are at work in New York City, where a person on a bike can often cross town faster than a car.

Riding the Rails

It didn't take cyclists long to discover that they could roll very easily over the smooth, level tracks of a railroad. Rail bikes became very popular in the 1800s. Whole families would pack a picnic lunch and go for a spin—on Sundays, that is, when the trains weren't running. Today, people are rediscovering pedal-powered rail vehicles. Riders can take advantage of thousands of miles of abandoned tracks, no longer used by trains.

The Railcycle is an ordinary mountain bike that balances on top of one rail, with the help of an arm that reaches out to the second rail. The arm can be folded out of the way for riding on the ground. Ron's Rider is a bit steadier. This two-person railcar has four wheels.

The young actor Henry Thomas pedals a Railcycle in the movie The Quest.

*From Switzerland comes the Villiger,
a streamlined bike for everyday use.*

*The Brike is a recumbent tricycle with
wide tires for riding off the road.*

HPVs You Can Buy

Few of us will buy a little streamlined rocket on wheels—
at least not until they become both cheaper and easier to drive.
For now, you can buy a recumbent bike without streamlining
for a lot less. Expect to pay 50 percent above the price of a
regular bike of the same quality. These prices should come
down in the future, as recumbents become popular and more
of them are made.

Above: This French trike carries its own built-in shopping cart.
Below: The Renegade is one of the very few recumbents made for smaller kids.

Above: The Danish Leitra is a pedal-powered tricycle for all kinds of weather. It has springs, as cars do, for a comfortable ride. Below: The Peach Ridge tricycle truck can be used as a golf cart.

3. *Pedal, Pedal, Pedal Your Boat*

Humans may be jackrabbits on land, but we're turtles in the water. Slower than turtles, in fact.

That's because water is thicker than air—about a thousand times thicker. What happens when you try to punch or kick underwater? Your arms and legs move as if you were in a slow-motion movie. And you've probably noticed that a three-year-old can run faster along the edge of a pool than you can possibly swim. You'll make better time if you hop into a canoe or rowboat. But humanpowered boats still aren't a match for a bicycle, which only has to push through air.

The fastest canoes, kayaks, and rowboats make the most of your power by cutting cleanly through the water. Their long and narrow bodies, called hulls, cause little of the rippling, splashing, or waves that are signs of wasted energy. If you are used to rowing tubby boats, you'd be amazed at how far you can go with just one pull on the oars of a racing rowboat, known as a shell. It feels as though the boat were being pulled by a hidden rope!

These shells owe their terrific speed, in part, to being long, sleek, and skinny. But they make the most of the rowers' strength in other clever ways. The seats slide back and forth on rails, allowing the legs to add their power and lengthening each stroke of the oars. And the oars pivot outside the hull of the shell, on outriggers. This gives rowers more leverage, so they can push against the water with greater force.

That sounds good, but there's a better way—using the legs to turn pedals attached to an underwater propeller. Rowers

The Alden Ocean Shell isn't as streamlined as a racing shell, but it can still row circles around most rowboats.

waste energy when they slide back and forth, because it's tiring to change direction after each stroke. And oars push entirely backward for only part of their stroke; the rest of the time they waste still more energy by pushing water somewhat to the side. You can demonstrate this for yourself. Place your arms out to the side like a pair of oars and move them back and forth in a rowing motion. Note that your hands face directly backward only when your arms are straight out to either side.

Even so, eight highly trained Olympic athletes can row 15 miles per hour in a modern shell. That's impressive. But consider this: Six French women pedaled that fast in a watercycle more than a hundred years ago, without the advantages of modern materials and training methods.

People forgot about the watercycles of the 1800s. But good ideas tend to come round again. Pedal-powered boats have caught the imagination of a new generation of people who like to travel over the water as fast as they can.

The *Flying Fish*

One of today's watercycle pioneers is Allan Abbott, a California physician. Abbott likes speed. He was the rider mentioned in chapter 2 who pedaled a bike 138 miles per hour behind a car that shielded him from the wind. So you can understand that he might be impatient with ordinary canoes and rowboats.

Abbott wanted to build a watercycle that would speed along on underwater wings called hydrofoils. Powerful ships have used hydrofoils to avoid the drag of their hulls in water. They can go faster riding *over* the water than bulldozing *through* it.

The Flying Fish *is the world's fastest humanpowered boat.*
Photo © 1985 by Randa Bishop.

But no one had ever managed the trick of doing that with humanpower. That's because a boat has to be traveling very fast in order to rise on its hydrofoils.

Abbott came up with a way to reach that speed—he decided to simply forget about having a hull. Instead, he would try launching his watercycle from a dock. That way he would hit the water going fast enough to stay up on hydrofoils.

Abbott's watercycle, the *Flying Fish*, was more a bicycle than a boat. He started with the frame from a ten-speed bike and added hydrofoils at the front and back. The pedals were attached to a propeller, instead of a rear wheel. The result looked like no other boat on Earth. Would the *Fish* fly on its water wings, or sink?

One day when the water was calm, the *Flying Fish* was placed on its launching platform. The platform would ride down a ramp on little skateboard wheels to get the *Fish* up to speed. Abbott climbed on board. He strapped his feet to the pedals. The countdown began: five, four, three. . . . At the count of one, Abbott began pedaling furiously, and at zero the platform pitched him forward, out onto the lake. The *Fish* was up on its hydrofoils, flying on the water. Abbott didn't feel like he was going very fast—the *Fish* splashed very little, and the ride was strangely quiet. But, in fact, he was going more quickly than he had hoped.

To judge his speed, Abbott had placed a tube on the *Fish* that ran up from the water to a clear section he could see. The faster he went, the higher the water would rise in the tube. Leaving the ramp, Abbott saw by marks on the tube that he was doing 7 or 8 miles per hour. He pedaled harder, got up to 13, and then went all out in a sprint. The water squirted right out the top of the tube!

Since that first flight, Abbott and his *Flying Fish* have gone on to break world speed records and earn a listing in the *Guiness Book of World Records*. The *Fish* is the fastest single-person boat, capable of nearly 20 miles per hour. On later models, pontoons were added to the frame so that a rider could begin anywhere from a standing start. Pontoons also keep the water-cycle from sinking at the end of its ride.

Fast but Not Tippy

Most high-speed boats are tricky to use. Racing shells are tippy. The *Flying Fish* takes a lot of energy if the rider is to stay up on hydrofoils. But other new pedal-powered designs are

The Saber Craft has a comfortable chair that sits on top of a narrow hull. A small pontoon keeps the boat from flipping over.

Above: The Waterbug looks like a tiny car that drives into the drink. A gear shift inside allows the rider to pedal at a comfortable rate, no matter what the speed. Steamlining allows the Waterbug to cruise at 5 miles per hour, even into waves and strong winds. Below: The Paddlever needs a crew of three—two to turn the paddlewheels, a third to steer. Photo © 1985 by Randa Bishop.

Above: The Hydro-ped looks like a normal kayak—until the rider pedals hard and the boat climbs up on its hydrofoils. Below: This two-person HPV may be funny looking, but it has an unusual ability: It can travel to the edge of a lake. . . and keep on going.

both easy and fun to operate. The rider faces front, unlike in a rowboat. And because the legs are the engine, the hands are free to steer, fish, or hold binoculars.

Quicker Canoes and Kayaks

Pedal power seems to be the wave of the future. But many builders continue to improve boats that are traditional in their part of the world.

In the Adirondack Mountains of New York State, builder Peter Hornbeck makes his Lost Pond canoes so light that they can be carried in one hand, like a suitcase. That means they are

The Lost Pond canoe weighs just nine pounds—a little more than a gallon of the stuff it floats in.

fast and easy to turn, like water-going sports cars. It also means that you can carry one into a lonely pond where boats may never have gone before. Hornbeck says he was inspired by the tiny wooden boats used by Nesmuk, the famous canoeist of the 1800s.

Hornbeck's boats aren't made of wood, however. He uses Kevlar, a strong fabric used in everything from cars to tennis racquets. The fabric is coated with a smooth layer of plastic for a hull that slips easily through the water. The canoeist slips through the air quite easily, too. That's because you paddle this boat sitting down on the floor; in ordinary canoes and rowboats, the body is upright, and it acts as a sail. Another advantage of these little boats is that they are narrow enough to power with a two-bladed paddle. Because strokes switch from one side to the other, the boat goes straight without the energy-wasting corrections that are needed to steer a larger canoe.

Washington State boat builder George Dyson is fascinated by another Native American boat, the kayak. He heard that European explorers in Alaska used to see Aleut Indians cruising at 10 miles per hour in their skin-covered kayaks. That's twice the cruising speed of today's fiberglass kayaks. What made these boats so fast?

Searching for the answer, Dyson has come across several mysteries. The bow (front end) of some Aleut boats was split in two. Could this give an advantage over the pointy bows of ordinary kayaks? The wooden frame was flexible, something like the skeleton of an animal. Did it allow the kayaks to flow over the waves more swiftly? The skin covering was flexible, too. Could that cut down on drag? This last question may not be answerable. To study the flow of liquids around a hull, scientists

Aleut kayaks in the water off the Alaska coast.

come up with math problems that even supercomputers aren't yet able to handle. So how could the Aleuts have managed to create such a fast, low-drag hull? Dyson guesses it was the result of tinkering with boats for two thousand years.

Dyson is now trying to build a modern kayak that will take advantage of the same unusual design. He'll need a good pair of arms, too, if he is to paddle at a steady 10 miles per hour: Recent studies of an Aleut kayaker who was mummified 900 years ago show that he had developed astoundingly large muscles from paddling.

Subs with Muscles

Today we tend to think of submarines as war machines. But they can be used for peaceful explorations as well. The Dive Cycle is as simple as a submarine could be. It works something like a sideways pogo stick with pedals. There is no hull whatsoever. To ride it, you use a mask and a snorkel or air tanks for air. The pedals are attached to a twelve-inch fan at one end. Two fins at the other end can be set to steer the sub.

More than two centuries after the Turtle *plopped into the sea, inventors are again making humanpowered submarines—but for fun and exploration, not to sink ships.*
Photo © 1984 by Randa Bishop.

The Squid *travels at 3 miles per hour, and
can dive to 25 feet below the surface.*

The world's first submarine race was held off the coast of
Florida in 1989. All of the seventeen machines were humanpowered. The winner was the U.S. Naval Academy's two-person
sub, the *Squid*. It is just eleven feet long and three feet across.
Unlike the *Turtle*, the world's first submarine, there's no air in
the cabin, and the riders have to wear air tanks.

4. *Birdmen and Birdwomen*

Humans have tried for centuries to fly with their own power. It took a money prize, offered in 1959, to get the job done. Henry Kremer, a British factory owner who loved airplanes, said he would give a big reward for the first humanpowered plane that could fly around a one-mile course in the shape of a figure-eight. Hundreds of people in several countries got to work. But, as in earlier attempts, everyone failed.

Sixteen years passed before a California engineer, Paul MacCready, Jr., decided he would try to win the prize. MacCready had built all sorts of model planes as a kid—not just the usual paper airplanes and balsa kits but helicopters and ornithopters, too.

Now as an adult, MacCready again turned to model making to try out his ideas. Like designers in centuries before him, he took his inspiration from nature. He knew that many of the features of today's most advanced airplanes were already in use by birds and bats, including refueling in midair, radar, long-distance navigation, and adjustable wing surfaces.

When he had a design he liked, he gathered a team of experts to make a full-sized plane of aluminum, balsa wood, Mylar plastic, tape, piano wire, and nylon shoelaces. The team worked in a huge building where floats were made for the Rose Bowl Parade. They needed the space: the plane they pieced together had a wingspan of ninety feet. It was big, but more delicate than a butterfly. The plane fell apart without ever taking off.

The *Gossamer Condor*

Then came months of trying to build a plane that was stronger but not heavier. Some of the parts were made by hand, with space-age materials. Others were very simple. The tiny landing wheels for one plane were taken from a toy fire engine!

Every unneeded ounce was shaved away. The bicycle parts that turned the propeller were drilled full of holes to make them lighter. The team's motto was, If it doesn't break, it's too heavy.

While working on planes, Paul MacCready and his two sons had also been working on themselves. They pedaled on an exercise machine to get in shape to be the pilots—and the engines—of the new plane. But MacCready decided a plane should have the strongest possible pilot, and he chose Bryan Allen, a champion bicyclist who happened to enjoy hang gliding.

In 1977, after many test runs and one crash, Allen pedaled a plane called the *Gossamer Condor* through a mile-long course and won the Kremer prize for the team. The flight took more than seven minutes—some readers of this book can *run* a one-mile course faster than that. But the *Condor* had earned the

The Gossamer Condor *was the world's first successful humanpowered plane.*

reputation as the world's first humanpowered plane. Today you can see it in Washington, D.C., hanging from the ceiling of the Smithsonian's National Air and Space Museum.

The *Condor*'s flight was impressive. But could a pilot-powered plane fly long distances, the way birds and other planes do?

The *Gossamer Albatross*

Henry Kremer wanted to find out. He offered a second prize, bigger than the first. It would be awarded to the first humanpowered plane to fly over the English Channel between

The Gossamer Albatross *crossed the English Channel.*

England and France. That would be a good test. The channel is twenty miles across at its narrowest. A plane that couldn't make the distance would crash into the sea.

Paul MacCready and his team developed the *Gossamer Albatross* for the flight. It weighed fifteen pounds less than the seventy-pound *Condor*. And yet it was strong—so strong that the plastic body was slit in places with a razor blade, just in case the pilot had to break out of it in a crash.

MacCready figured that the pilot would need to put out one-half horsepower to take off and a bit less to cruise over the Channel. Pilot Bryan Allen could generate more power by turning pedals with his arms as well as his legs. But controlling the *Albatross* over the sea would be tricky enough, and the team decided to leave the pilot's arms free to steer the plane.

Allen was given several instruments. A tiny windmill sent signals to a gauge that told the plane's speed through the air. Another gauge told how fast the pedals were spinning. A thermometer gave the temperature in the cabin. Finally, he was guided by an altimeter made from an electric eye taken from a self-focusing camera. It told how high the plane was above the water. That was important information. Pilots have a hard time judging how far they are above a smooth sea, and they can get dangerously close. Bryan Allen even had a very simple form of air-conditioning. He could yank strings attached to flaps in the airplane's skin to let in fresh air.

The *Albatross* took off early one morning in 1979, skimming just above the waves. Some three pounds of dew was sitting on its wings, which meant that Bryan Allen had to pedal harder than usual. Then a wind came up, slowing the plane still more. With just six miles to go, Allen felt he could pedal no farther.

The Bionic Bat *takes off. The pilot stores energy before a flight by turning the pedals to make electricity. This power runs a motor that helps spin the propeller. Photo © 1984 by Randa Bishop.*

He radioed the boats below that he was giving up. But as Allen climbed to fifteen feet above the sea in order to get a tow from a boat, the air became smoother. He decided to keep on going.

Almost three hours after takeoff, the *Gossamer Albatross* landed on the French shore. Bryan Allen was completely exhausted. He said that if the beach had been just 300 feet farther, he would have crashed into the sea.

Flying Faster and Farther

The *Gossamer* planes could go long distances, but they took their time in getting there. New Kremer prizes had been offered to encourage the design of faster planes. In 1983 Paul Mac-

Cready's son Parker flew a plane called the *Bionic Bat* around a course at a record speed of 27 miles per hour. The *Bat* had an unusual feature. The pilot pedaled an electric generator before takeoff and stored the energy in batteries aboard the plane. This power was then used to help turn the propeller in flight.

The MacCreadys aren't the only successful people in this story. In 1988 another team attempted to duplicate Daedalus's flight from the island of Crete, mentioned in chapter 1. The plane would have to take off from Crete and travel seventy-four miles over the sea. Also named the *Daedalus*, it had an amazing wingspan of 112 feet—four feet longer than that of a Boeing 727 jet. Greek bicycling champion Kanellos Kanellopoulos was the pilot. On the morning of the flight, he appeared in racing shorts cut full of holes—his humorous way of helping the team cut down on the plane's weight!

Kanellos took off perfectly and had no trouble pedaling an average speed of 19 miles per hour. As he neared shore, a sharp wind came up. Kanellos struggled to land on the beach. But a gust snapped part of the tail, and the *Daedalus* fell into the sea, tearing its great wing to pieces. Kanellos got a dunking, but he was overjoyed—the team had succeeded in setting a new world distance record.

What's It Like To Pedal a Plane?

The newest humanpowered airplanes aren't that difficult to pilot if the wind is still. Most people in good shape can fly them short distances, teenagers and those in their sixties, men and women.

Believe it or not, one of the trickiest parts of a flight is

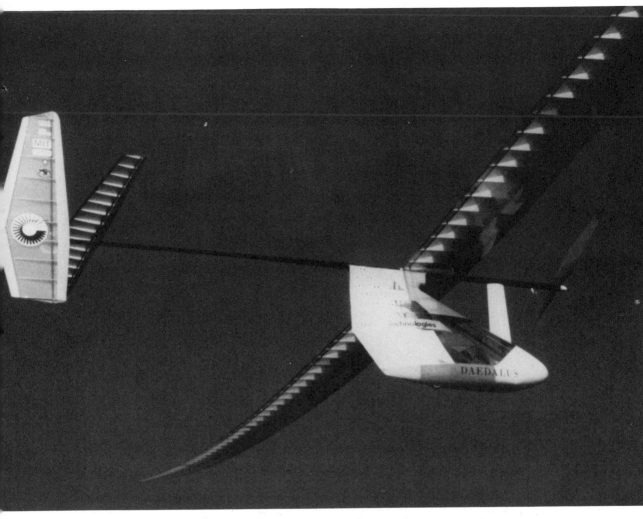

To people watching Daedalus *from below, the pilot's pumping legs look like the heartbeat of this enormous plastic bird.*

simply getting inside the plane. To avoid putting your weight on a fragile part and breaking it, you need help when climbing into the cabin. Once inside, you make sure your safety helmet is secure. Then you pedal hard to gain speed for the takeoff. Flying is so smooth that you might not realize you've left the ground. But it's surprisingly noisy up there, because of the revolving bicycle parts and the *whoosh* of the propeller.

To climb higher into the sky, all you do is pedal harder. To lose altitude, you just take it easy. But not *too* easy. If air isn't passing fast enough over the long wings, the plane may drop very quickly and crash. Gusts are another problem. They have caused crashes by slowing the flow of air over the wings. And the wind can break parts right off the plane. That's why today's humanpowered pilots keep poor Icarus in mind and stay close to the ground for safety's sake.

Landing is easy. All you do is line the plane up with the runway and pedal more slowly.

Pedal-Powered Helicopters

It seems so simple! Hook pedals to a big fan that points at the sky, and up you go. Leonardo da Vinci designed the first

Lift off! Da Vinci III *becomes the world's first humanpowered helicopter to leave the ground.*

humanpowered helicopter. But that bit of progress was followed by five hundred years of failure.

No one managed to leave the ground until 1989, when a team of students at California Polytechnic State University finally beat gravity. Their copter, appropriately named *Da Vinci III*, is propelled by a pilot sitting in a recumbent seat. It took nine years of designing and testing to make a very short flight—just seven seconds long and eight inches above the ground. The pilot could have gone higher but had to ease up on the pedals. This test flight was performed in a gymnasium with the basketball backboards hoisted out of the way. The *Da Vinci III* is too fragile to fly in even a slight breeze.

Pedal-Powered Blimps

Pedal-powered planes are getting faster and faster. But speed isn't everything, according to Bryan Allen, who was the pilot on the historic runs of the *Condor* and *Albatross*. Some of the new planes are trickier to handle and just not that much fun, he says. He prefers the easy riding provided by a pedal-powered blimp.

A blimp is a lighter-than-air vehicle. That means the pilot doesn't have to work to keep it aloft. All of his or her muscle power can be used to go forward.

The idea of a humanpowered blimp is nothing new. In France two hundred years ago, Jean-Pierre Blanchard made one by attaching a propeller to a balloon. A modern version is the *White Dwarf*, which was first pumped up and sent aloft in 1985. It is roughly the size of a small house. The pilot can pedal at 8 or 10 miles per hour without working too hard, and top speed

Above: Pedaling the White Dwarf *blimp is something like riding a bike, but the view is better. Below: Strong winds make the* White Dwarf *bob around like a huge party balloon. An inexperienced pilot can't fly it safely in breezes over 3 miles per hour. Photos © 1984 by Randa Bishop.*

is about 14. To go up, you tilt the propeller downward, just as you would adjust a fan. To go down or to land, you tilt the propeller up.

A big rudder guides the blimp through slow and easy turns. To make a tighter turn, though, the pilot uses a small propeller that is aimed to the side. With this propeller, the *White Dwarf* can fly around inside a large gymnasium.

That sounds like great fun. But don't expect to see many people building big, fat garages for their blimps. The *White Dwarf* isn't nearly as practical as a bicycle or car. It cost nearly $40,000 to design and build. And even though the blimp doesn't use any fuel, it's expensive to operate. The bag holds about $600 worth of helium gas, and $2 of that leaks out every day.

Is There a Future for Humanpowered Flight?

As you can see, humanpowered planes and blimps are expensive, fragile machines. Designer Paul MacCready says a sturdy, safe plane would need at least 3 horsepower to handle its weight. And yet even an excellent bicyclist can average only one-tenth of that.

Still, these experimental flights have led the way for engine-powered planes that can fly on a tiny amount of energy. Paul MacCready found that solar cells on the wings can generate enough power for long flights. He developed the first solar plane, the *Gossamer Penguin*, in 1980. The following year, his *Solar Challenger* flew 163 miles at an altitude of 11,000 feet— without burning one drop more of petroleum fuel than an eagle would have. MacCready says he hopes to design a plane that can fly around the world on a few gallons of gas.

Why bother? Paul MacCready himself admits his fantastic machines aren't practical. He explains, "A while ago I realized that many of the people in this country are willing to send my kids to war so they can keep driving the same cars they've been driving instead of solving the problems of energy. I asked myself what I could do to help decrease the country's dependence on foreign oil."

So pedaling your own body around might have an influence on world peace! That's something to think about, next time you hop on your bike rather than ask for a ride in a car.

5. *Make Your Own Humanpowered Vehicle*

To build a record-breaking humanpowered vehicle, you need many thousands of dollars and years of technical training—and probably the help of a lot of experienced people, too. But there are less expensive ways to experiment with going faster under your own power. Here are some ideas you might try, as well as a few products you can purchase.

Brisker Biking

When you pedal fast on a bicycle, the wind in your face cools you off. But you pay a price for this air-conditioning—the wind is slowing you down and making you work harder. Remember, above 10 miles per hour most of your muscle power is used to push through the air. You can do several things to slip through it more easily.

The simplest is to duck down. Some handlebars are designed to let you lean low to the wind. Drop bars—those found on touring and racing bikes—allow you to hold on either sitting upright or bending down low. In the lower position, you can cut your wind resistance by at least 20 percent. If your bike has regular flat bars, think about changing to drop bars. Prices for them vary a lot, from inexpensive steel bars to those made of costly lightweight alloys. Bike shops either sell drop bars or can order them for you. They're easy to install, although you'll also have to remove and reattach brake and gearshift levers.

But before you switch to drop bars, try riding a bike that has them. Are you comfortable in the lower position? Some riders don't enjoy hunching over. Their backs hurt from leaning, or their necks hurt from keeping their chins up. In fact, many people whose bikes came with drop bars have switched to *regular* bars; these riders are happy to trade less wind resistance for more comfort.

You can wedge your body through the air still more easily with aero handlebars. Perhaps you've noticed Greg Lemond and other bicycle racers using them. To install aero bars, you just bolt them onto the handlebars you have now.

Another easy way to cut more easily through the air is to wear snug clothes. Take a look through a bicycling magazine, and you'll see that racers and even everyday riders wear body-suits that fit more like a shiny coat of paint than clothing. These items are available through some bike shops and by mail through bicycling magazines. You don't have to buy a special wardrobe, though. Just pick out clothes that are both somewhat snug and also flexible enough to allow free movement. A large, blousy jacket is *not* the sort of thing to wear, especially if you leave it open to catch the wind like a sail. Even the material

The human head is already a streamlined object, but a helmet has still less wind resistance, and will protect you in a fall.

matters. A smooth fabric will slip through the air a little better than rough wool, for example.

Does your bike have bags for carrying cargo? They're a great help at times. But consider removing them when you don't need to carry cargo. Their weight and wind resistance slow you down. Even though a water bottle doesn't create much drag, you can give yourself a slight edge by mounting it behind your seat, rather than out in the wind on the frame below the seat.

Bicycle designers try to make their machines go faster by trimming every possible fraction of an ounce. So it may seem odd that one good way to gain another mile or two per hour is to *add* something to your bike—a streamlined nose. These noses, called fairings, work by directing air smoothly around you and your bike. Some fairings have built-in compartments for storing things. This can give you an added boost, as it means you won't have to attach bulky storage bags to your bike. If you can't find fairings at your local bicycle shop, ask about ordering one.

Large fairings do the best job, because they direct more air. But they are heavier and cost more than smaller fairings. Even small fairings aren't inexpensive. Some cost as much as an inexpensive bike itself! So before buying one you should ask yourself how important streamlining will be to you.

Do you spend much time at speeds above 15 miles per

The Aerocarrier fairing looks good. It also cuts wind drag 10 percent. This means you can pedal 21 miles per hour with the same power it would take you to go 20 without a fairing.

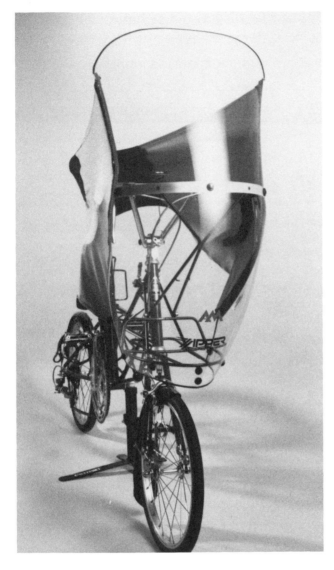

This AM Zzipper fairing wraps around the rider. It was made especially for the tiny-wheeled AM, a bike that comes apart in the middle and can be carried in a bag.

hour? If the answer is no, then a fairing probably won't be worth its price and its added weight. That's made clear by the following table (these figures are for the Aerocarrier fairing, made by National Cycle). At 20 miles per hour, this fairing reduces air resistance by more than 20 percent. That means you'd be able to go almost 1 mile per hour faster without pedaling any harder. But the slower you travel, the less of a problem wind resistance will be and the less value you'll get from a fairing.

How Much Speed Will a Fairing Give You?

At this speed (mph)...	15	20	25	30
...you'll go this much faster	.7	.9	1.1	1.4

A fiberglass disk wheel cover will increase your top speed by 3 percent. A little flap opens so that you can pump the tire.

The wheels of your bike are like fans—they spin and churn up the wind, and this slows you down. You can buy wheels with fewer spokes and even one that has just three streamlined spokes. These will give you a small advantage. But at prices between $100 and ten times that much, you aren't getting a lot of miles per hour for the money. Another choice is to attach a disk to a wheel. This is faster still, but a disk on the front wheel can act like a sail in a crosswind and make steering difficult. For that reason it's best to use a disk on the back wheel only.

Don't forget to check the pressure of your tires. If they are low on air, they are creating more friction than they need to. Pump them up to the recommended pressure, and you'll roll more easily.

Get Your Arms into the Act

Have you noticed that bicycle racers tend to be built something like frogs? They have muscular thighs and thin arms. That's because pedaling a bicycle is great for the legs, but other parts of the body go along for the ride.

Your arms can do more than just keep you from falling off the bike. A Florida inventor has come out with Ultra Mac, a pair of handlebars that are rowed to power the front wheel. The bars are connected to the wheel by a chain and even have their own set of gears. This device isn't a toy. It is well made and costs about as much as a bicycle itself. The inventor says that you can get 31 percent more power out of your bicycle with his system. A bike shop should be able to install it in about half an hour.

Ultra Mac handlebars are rowed to power the front wheel.

Recumbent Bikes

If you really are serious about making good speed, think about switching to a recumbent bike. The seat allows you to lean back and cause less drag.

Because most bike riders are unfamiliar with recumbents, few are made. And because few are made, prices are high. Not until factories are cranking out tens of thousands of recumbents will they cost the same as ordinary bikes. Some companies sell just the frame, so that buyers can save a bit of money by adding gears, pedals, brakes, and wheels from bikes they already own.

The fastest pedal-powered vehicles of all have full bodies. These are the HPVs that look like little cars and the ones that set world speed records. Unfortunately, they are rarely for sale, and they aren't easy to build. Designing a streamlined body takes a lot of knowledge. Building one demands working with a lightweight material—plastic, metal, or cloth—that will take on the smooth shapes of the design.

You might be able to find someone to help you build an HPV with a fairing or complete body. Try going through your school, scouting organization, or local chapter of the International Humanpowered Vehicle Association (see "For More Information," following this chapter). A number of high schools have made and raced their own vehicles. Some of the best humanpowered cars, boats, and planes are built by college engineering students.

You don't have to use expensive space-age materials. Some designers get by with sheets of cardboard, plastic, and aluminum. The results probably won't look as sleek as a race car, but

This homemade prototype isn't very pretty. But its designer, James Donohue, cleverly used inexpensive materials to experiment with air resistance.

you may end up with a faster bike. These one-of-a-kind designs are called prototypes. Large car and airplane manufacturers make them, too, when planning new models. Even if a prototype is patched together with tape and string, it can be an excellent way to try out your ideas.

Boats You Can Build or Buy

A boat is the simplest sort of humanpowered vehicle you can make. It doesn't have to have any moving parts—just a hull to keep you afloat while you pedal, paddle, or stroke. Hulls can be made of a great number of materials, including strips of

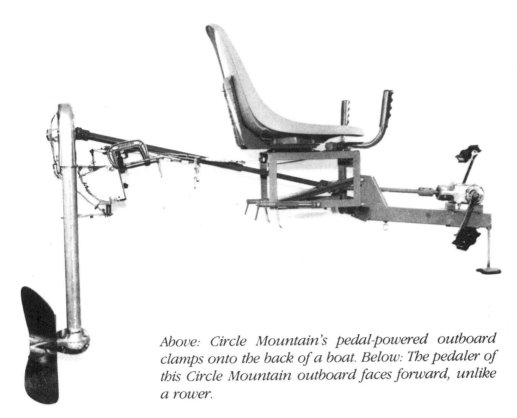

Above: Circle Mountain's pedal-powered outboard clamps onto the back of a boat. Below: The pedaler of this Circle Mountain outboard faces forward, unlike a rower.

wood that are glued together, plywood sheets, aluminum, and many kinds of plastic.

This isn't to say that boatbuilding takes no skill. You've got to be able to follow plans and instructions. You should have experience with hand tools and be responsible enough to handle the toxic and flammable glues and resins involved in making a hull. For the addresses of magazines with articles on boatbuilding, see the section following this chapter.

It is simpler, of course, to rent or buy a boat. Boat-rental companies may have kayaks, lightweight canoes, and racing shells that you can try. They may also sell used high-performance boats at the end of the vacation season.

A small company in Montana has come up with a way to make ordinary canoes and rowboats speedier. It's a pedal-powered outboard! The outboard comes complete with a comfortable seat for you, the engine. The pedals turn a shaft, which spins a propeller behind the boat. With this outboard, a canoe can hit a top speed of almost 6 miles per hour.

A Do-It-Yourself Airplane?

Planes are the trickiest vehicles of all to design, build, and fly. Many details have to be worked out if the plane is to have a chance of leaving the ground. And, once off the ground, the plane faces the challenge of not crashing back into it.

Still, you can learn to help make and fly humanpowered planes. The graceful wings of the *Gossamer Albatross* and *Daedalus* owe a lot to math and science. The school courses you take now may seem a world away from that sort of excitement.

But they can give you the background you'll need to understand and design such marvelous machines in a few years from now. Much of the best work in humanpowered transportation is being done at colleges, by students not much older than you. So stick with your math and science classes. Unless you take the trouble to learn the basics now, it will be difficult to master them later if you decide to go into a technical field.

For More Information

Want to find out more? Here are several publications and groups that can help you. If your library doesn't have a book you want, ask if it can be loaned through another library.

Magazines and Newsletters

HPV News and *Human Power*. The members' newsletter and journal of the International Human Powered Vehicle Association. P.O. Box 51255, Indianapolis, Indiana 46215.

Recumbent Cyclist. Newsletter about recumbent bicycling. 16621 123rd Avenue, S.E., Renton, Washington 98058.

Bicycling. Articles on regular racing and mountain bikes. Rodale Press, Inc., 33 E. Minor Street, Emmaus, Pennsylvania 18098.

WoodenBoat. Ideas and plans for fast, lightweight rowboats, canoes, and kayaks, as well as larger boats. P.O. Box 78, Brooklin, Maine 04616.

Books

Bicycles and Tricycles, by Archibald Sharp (Cambridge, Massachusetts: The MIT Press, 1977). Not many books are still being printed a hundred years after they were written. But bike designers continue to use this one, first published in 1896, for information, and the pictures of strange old bikes are fun to see.

Bicycling Science, by Frank Roland Whitt and David Gordon Wilson (Cambridge, Massachusetts: The MIT Press, 1982). Two engineers give a technical (but interesting) explanation of how bikes work and how they can be improved.

Gossamer Odyssey, by Morton Grosser (Boston, Massachusetts: Houghton Mifflin, 1981). The story of Paul MacCready's quest for humanpowered flight.

The History of Man-Powered Flight, by David A. Reay (Oxford, England: Pergamon Press, 1977). Tells about earlier attempts to fly.

Index

Among the many people and groups who helped gather the pictures for this book are Jan Vandertuin, Marti Daily, Jean Seay, Bob Flower, Chet Kyle, Paul MacCready, Mike Eliasohn, Tim Brummer, Randa Bishop, Michael Chritton, James Guilford, David Gordon Wilson, Jake Free, Peter Bohr, Richard Smart, the Institute for Transportation and Development Policy, the Adirondack Museum, and Rodale Stock Images. Special thanks to David Gordon Wilson for reviewing the manuscript for accuracy.

Illustration credits: page 16(top), Smithsonian Institution photo; page 16(bottom), National Archives; page 17, Burlington County (NJ) Cultural and Heritage Commission; page 18, courtesy of the Adirondack Museum; page 19, courtesy of Wolfgang Gronen, Intern. Rad- und Flugsport-Archiv, Binningen, Germany; page 22, Aeh T. Tem; pages 29, 40(bottom), © by Schmitz Mochet, Liou-Gordes, France; page 38, courtesy of the Internat'l Human Powered Vehicle Ass'n (IHPVA); pages 39, 83, Zzip Designs, Davenport, CA; page 41, James Guilford; pages 44, 84, Lightning Cycle Dynamics, Lompoc, CA; page 45, Peter Britton; page 46, courtesy of Jan Vandertuin, Human-powered Machines, Eugene, OR; page 47, Libby Photographers, Spokane, WA; page 49, Mike Lofgren; page 50(top), Automobiles Gateau, Ivry Sur Seine, France; page 50(bottom), Ed Roeters, Alternative Bikestyles, Bonita, CA; page 51(top), Marti Daily, IHPVA; page 51(bottom), Peach Ridge Petal Power, Athens, OH; page 53, Martin Marine Co., Kittery Point, ME; page 57, Jon Knapp; page 58(top) Garry Hoyt, Newport R&D, Newport, RI; page 59(top), Sid Shutt; page 60, Peter Hornbeck, Lost Pond Boats, Olmsteadville, NY; page 62, Alaska State Museum; page 64, Perry Fdn.; pages 67, 68–69, AeroVironment, Inc.; page 73, MIT photo; page 74, Cal Poly photo by Douglas Johnson Photographers; page 81, Vetta Helmets; page 82, Aerocarrier; page 86, Ultra Mac Corp., Miami, FL; page 88, James Donohue; page 89, Circle Mountain Industries, Fort Benton, MT.